Timeline of Egyptian Pyramids

ca. 2700 B.C.

Step Pyramid is built at Saqqara for Pharaoh Djoser.

ca. 2350 B.C.

Pyramid is built for Pharaoh Unas. This is one of the first pyramids to be decorated inside.

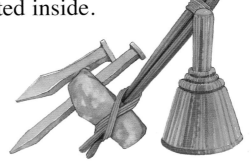

ca. 2300 B.C.

Pyramid building stops because of political instability.

ca. 2600 B.C.

"Bent" Pyramid is built at Dahshur. In the middle of construction the builders must have decided that the slope of the building was too steep to continue, so they gave the top half of the pyramid a shallower slope. North (or Red) Pyramid is built at Dahshur for Pharaoh Snefru. This is the first pyramid built in the "true" pyramid shape.

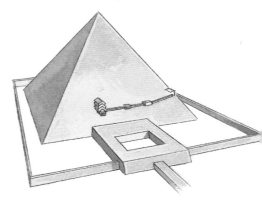

ca. 440 B.C.

Greek writer Herodotus visits Egypt and writes about the pyramids.

ca. 1790 B.C.

The pharaohs of ancient Egypt stop building pyramids. New Kingdom pharaohs are buried in rock-cut tombs.

1798

Napoleon Bonaparte leads his army into Egypt. He brings a team of scientists with him to study the pyramids and other ancient remains.

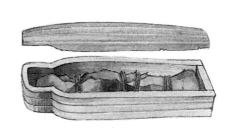

ca. 2000 B.C.

Pyramid building resumes at the beginning of the Middle Kingdom.

ca. A.D. 1700

European travelers and explorers begin exploring pyramids.

ca. 1300 B.C.

Khaemwaset (one of the sons of Ramses II) restores the pyramid of Unas.

Map of the Pyramids

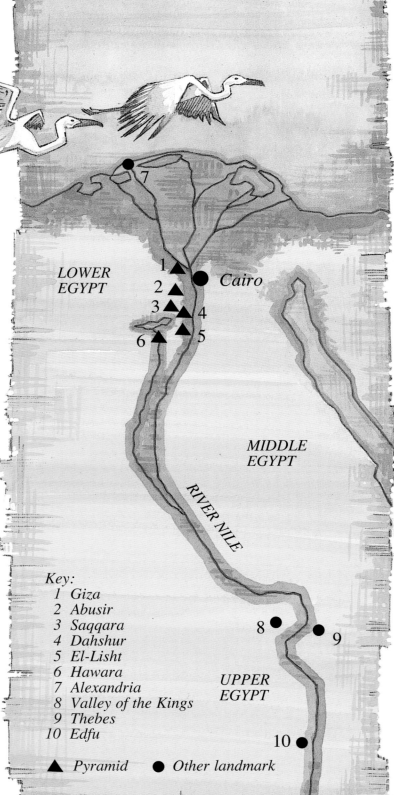

ncient Egypt's recorded history spans more than three thousand years, from about 3100 B.C. until 30 B.C., when Egypt became part of the Roman Empire. Egyptologists divide this long stretch of time into several periods, calling the three most important ones the Old, Middle, and New kingdoms. The great age of pyramid building was during the Old Kingdom (2686–2181 B.C.), when the Great Pyramid of Giza was built. Many later pyramids also survive, but mostly as crumbling heaps of rubble. The map at right depicts a small selection of Egypt's famous pyramid sites and other landmarks.

LOWER EGYPT

Cairo

MIDDLE EGYPT

RIVER NILE

UPPER EGYPT

Key:
 1 Giza
 2 Abusir
 3 Saqqara
 4 Dahshur
 5 El-Lisht
 6 Hawara
 7 Alexandria
 8 Valley of the Kings
 9 Thebes
10 Edfu

▲ Pyramid   ● Other landmark

Author:
Jacqueline Morley studied English at
Oxford University. She has taught English and
history, and has a special interest in the history of
everyday life. She is the author of numerous
children's books, including award-winning
historical nonfiction for children.

Artist:
David Antram was born in Brighton, England,
in 1958. He studied at Eastbourne College of Art
and then worked in advertising for 15 years before
becoming a full-time artist. He has illustrated
many children's nonfiction books.

Series Creator:
David Salariya was born in Dundee,
Scotland. He has illustrated a wide range of books
and has created and designed many new series for
publishers both in the UK and overseas. In 1989,
he established The Salariya Book Company. He
lives in Brighton with his wife, illustrator Shirley
Willis, and their son, Jonathan.

Editor:
Karen Barker Smith

Assistant Editor:
Michael Ford

© The Salariya Book Company Ltd MMXIV
No part of this publication may be reproduced in whole or in
part, or stored in a retrieval system, or transmitted in any form or
by any means, electronic, mechanical, photocopying, recording,
or otherwise, without written permission of the publisher. For
information regarding permission, write to the copyright holder.

Published in Great Britain in 2014 by
The Salariya Book Company Ltd
25 Marlborough Place, Brighton BN1 1UB

ISBN-13: 978-0-531-27101-8 (lib. bdg.) 978-0-531-23852-3 (pbk.)

All rights reserved.
Published in 2014 in the United States
by Franklin Watts
An imprint of Scholastic Inc.

A CIP catalog record for this book is available
from the Library of Congress.

Printed and bound in Heyuan, China.
Printed on paper from sustainable sources.
Reprinted in MMXXI.

15 16 17 18 R 25 24 23 22 21

SCHOLASTIC, FRANKLIN WATTS, and associated logos are
trademarks and/or registered trademarks of Scholastic Inc.,
557 Broadway, New York, NY 10012.

PAPER FROM
SUSTAINABLE
FORESTS

You Wouldn't Want to Be a
Pyramid Builder!

Written by
Jacqueline Morley

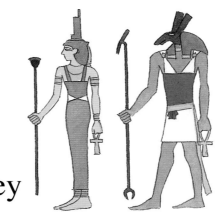

Illustrated by
David Antram

Created and designed by
David Salariya

A Hazardous Job You'd Rather Not Have

Franklin Watts®
An Imprint of Scholastic Inc.
NEW YORK • TORONTO • LONDON • AUCKLAND • SYDNEY
MEXICO CITY • NEW DELHI • HONG KONG
DANBURY, CONNECTICUT

Contents

Ra

Introduction

You are living in Egypt around 1500 B.C. How lucky you are! Other nations struggle to keep going, but Egypt is different—or so its people believe. Each year, as if by magic, Egypt's Nile River overflows its banks, watering the desert and dumping a belt of rich soil over the land. Without it, nothing would grow and everyone would starve. The Egyptians think the gods look after them because their rulers, the pharaohs, are gods themselves. When a pharaoh dies he joins the hawk-headed sun god Ra and travels the sky in his boat. To make sure he lives forever the pharaoh's corpse must not decay. So each pharaoh gets his subjects to build him a gigantic tomb—a pyramid—which will preserve his body forever. Thousands of Egyptians are forced to work on it, including you.

Mediterranean Sea

Delta

Limestone quarry

Red Sea

EGYPT

Nile River

Granite quarry

Scraping a Living

WHAT YOU OWN. You don't have much in the way of possessions—perhaps a pig, a goat, and some geese. Your furniture is just a few stools, boxes, and storage jars, and you sleep on a mat on the floor.

Some people in Egypt are very rich—the pharaoh and his court, high-ranking officials, and wealthy landowners—but the majority are poor. Some make a living by making things to sell, especially in the towns. Most people earn their keep by farming the land. As an ordinary Egyptian that's what you do. You grow crops for a rich landowner and in return he lets you have a patch of land to grow things on to feed your family. You have to work hard for him and hard for yourself, too.

Storage jars

Stool

Sleeping mat

Goat

Pig

Geese

WHERE YOU LIVE. Your little house is built of bricks made of sun-baked mud. Its flat roof gives your family a bit of extra living space.

For eight months you're hard at work, plowing, sowing, weeding, watering (it hardly ever rains), and harvesting. Then the Nile flood comes. For the rest of the year you can't farm because the land is under water. If you're expecting a rest, think again!

Handy Hint

Don't build your house on low ground or it will be under water in the flood season!

TILLING YOUR OWN PATCH. If you are too poor to own an ox, you and your family will have to pull the plow yourselves (left).

If you are really poor and don't even have a plow, you will have to dig your patch with a mattock (right).

Plow

Mattock

Officials, Officials

The pharaoh is all-powerful—the Egyptian people think he is a god. He has a very efficient government that makes sure his commands are carried out throughout the land. His officials keep records of who lives where and how wealthy they are. They come around every year to check that the figures are up to date. Then they decide how much tax you have to pay the pharaoh. Since the Ancient Egyptians haven't invented money, you pay this by handing over things you have produced or by doing work on official projects. The biggest official project is the pharaoh's pyramid, which will take years to finish. With all those farm laborers sitting idle in the flood season, the pharaoh doesn't have a problem finding workers. He sends his officials around the villages to call up people like you.

THE PHARAOH'S RING is his official stamp used to mark documents containing his orders.

Pharaoh's ring

What You Have to Put Up With

TAXES. At the start of the season, officials assess your tax by measuring the area you allocate to each crop in the current year.

PROBLEMS. If your crop is poor that year, or someone's cattle get loose and eat it, you still have to pay the amount that's been assessed.

REPAIRS. Before the flood comes, officials make you repair the canals that store the Nile's precious water for use throughout the year.

Pulling Your Weight

Now you're one of 4,000 people working on a pyramid which could take 20 years to build. As an unskilled worker your job is hauling blocks of stone from the quarry, where they're cut, to where the masons are waiting to set them in position. The pyramid is formed by layer upon layer of these blocks. Apart from the pharaoh's burial chamber and an entrance passage, the pyramid is solid stone throughout and requires over two million blocks. Working in a gang of 20, you drag stone higher and higher as the pyramid grows. Around 35 gangs have to deliver a block every two minutes, so the overseers keep you working hard. You work from sunrise to sunset, sleep in crowded barracks, and only get one day off in ten.

GIANT STATUES of the pharaoh will adorn a temple in his honor, which will be attached to the pyramid. One hundred and seventy-two men are needed to haul each one.

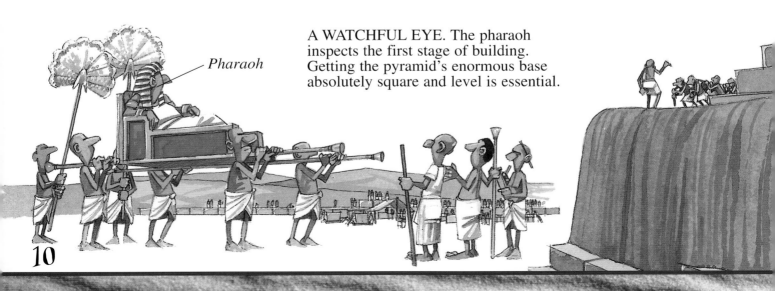

Pharaoh

A WATCHFUL EYE. The pharaoh inspects the first stage of building. Getting the pyramid's enormous base absolutely square and level is essential.

WAYS AROUND A PROBLEM.
The ancient Egyptians haven't invented wheeled vehicles. They use sledges to transport heavy objects. Laying a temporary runway of smooth logs makes it easier to slide the sledge over the ground.

Handy Hint
Your sledge will move more smoothly if the log path is coated with mud, kept slippery by you pouring water on it as you go.

HEAVE!

Block of stone   *Sledge*

At this stage in the building process the pyramid has stepped sides. It is very hard to haul stone up these steps so a temporary ramp has to be built. It is not known exactly how this looked, but here are two possibilities (right).

Temporary ramps are built around the pyramid.

Sent to the Quarries

f you are handy with a mallet and chisel you might find yourself in the stone quarries. The one near the site provides stone for the pyramid's core, but the fine limestone used for the outside surface comes from quarries east of the river. If you are sent there you'll be working underground, since the best stone lies beneath the surface. You chip blocks away at the top and sides and then split them free at the base with long wooden levers. It's backbreaking work, but not as grim as being sent to quarry granite in the far south of Egypt. It's boiling hot there and you work in the open, trying to cut into very hard rock with a lump of stone.

THE WORST FATE OF ALL. Granite, used for the decorative work, is extremely hard. It takes hours of effort to make a dent on it. You chip away with the pointed end of a heavy lump of dolerite, an even harder stone, but it soon gets blunt.

YOUR TOOLS include a wooden mallet, a stone-headed hammer, and chisels made of copper, which is the hardest metal available. (The Ancient Egyptians haven't invented iron working.)

Stone-headed hammer

Copper chisels

Wooden mallet

He must be new!

Skilled Stuff—Masons at Work

At the top of the ramp, teams of masons are putting the stones into position. This is a skilled job and if you are one of these workers you won't be a conscript, but a trained, full-time employee of the pharaoh. As each block is delivered it is checked for size and fit and levered into position with wooden rods. The outer casing blocks must fit together perfectly, but the masons must not take too long or there will be a pileup of blocks waiting to be set. When the last block, the pointed capstone, is in place, the ramp will be demolished from the top down. Then the edges of each layer are trimmed and polished to form a continuous slope.

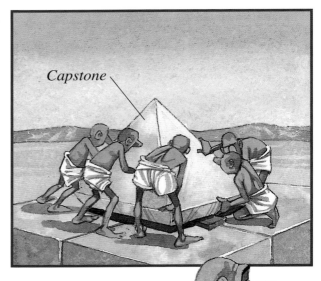

Capstone

THE FINAL PIECE. Setting the capstone in place is one of the trickiest jobs. There's not much room to maneuver. Mind your toes!

Plumbline and set-square to make sure blocks are level

Nearly there!

Scribes, Scribes, Scribes

The Pharaoh Knows Everything—How Does He Manage It?

Each day, the amount of work you do is recorded in writing by a professional record keeper, called a scribe. Most ordinary people do not know how to write, so being a scribe is a good career. There are scribes all over the site, keeping track of everything: the number of blocks delivered daily; the number laid; the tools issued in the morning and the number handed in at night; the delivery of food supplies; the rations issued; the reason for anyone's absence; and the cause of any accident or dispute. Their reports enable the site officials to keep a tight control on men and materials and if the work is on schedule. These officials report to their superiors, who report to theirs, on up the ranks, all the way to the pharaoh.

IN ALL OFFICIAL WORK, people report to their overseers. Scribes keep a record.

THE OVERSEERS report on the reports to their department heads.

THE DEPARTMENT HEADS report to the vizier, who is the pharaoh's chief minister.

THE VIZIER reports daily to the pharaoh on all that's happening in his kingdom.

Brush case

Dried ink

Writing brushes

Water pot

WRITING KIT. A scribe's tools include an oblong brush case for the brushes he writes with, a cake of dried ink, and a holder for water to moisten it.

Handy Hint
Don't try to "borrow" tools for your own use. You'll be searched if the records don't match.

Now make a careful note of this.

Carvers and Painters

Would you like a job inside? It might be claustrophobic and spooky working by lamplight deep inside a mountain of stone. To qualify you have to be highly skilled. The workers who decorate the pharaoh's burial chamber and funerary temple have had lengthy training. You need a sure hand to enlarge a complicated design to fill a large area of wall. You then carve away the background so that the figures are slightly raised. Finally, they are painted in their traditional colors. It is very important to know the exact stance and gestures the figures should portray and what symbols and written spells should accompany them. There are long-established rules about this. If you get any of them wrong the decorations will lose their magic power of ensuring the pharaoh's safe journey to the gods.

TYPICAL PYRAMID LAYOUT. The pyramid, with its mortuary temple against one side, stands in a walled enclosure. A causeway leads from the temple to the river.

Portcullis

Passageway

Burial chamber

Entrance

Mortuary temple

Causeway to river

Mixing paint

WALL PAINTERS help transfer the design to the wall. Both are marked with a grid. If you are just a trainee you'll be mixing the paint by grinding minerals to a powder and adding egg white or sticky tree resin.

18

19

Home Comforts

If you are a craftsmen working full-time for the pharaoh you'll be housed in a specially built town near the site. You and your family will have a small mud-brick house with a couple of rooms for living and sleeping, a storeroom, and an outside cooking area at the back. Your quarters are cramped and bare. The floor is beaten earth and the windows are small and high up to keep out the sun's glare. There is no comfortable furniture. Food, mainly coarse homemade bread, vegetables, and very little meat, is served on low tables. Cooking is done over a fire made in a hole in the ground.

Life in the Town

THE TOWN is protected by a wall with a gate that is guarded by day and shut at night.

MOST OF THE SUPPLIES the town needs are brought in on pack donkeys.

WATER has to be drawn from a reservoir outside the town gate.

SHOPPING without money needs bargaining skill. You pay in goods (known as bartering)—as few as possible.

ON PAY DAY, your wages come in various useful forms, such as grain, oil, or fine linen cloth.

CRAFTSMANSHIP is handed down within families. You'll want to train your son to follow you.

21

Staying on the Right Side of the Gods

Isis   *Seth*

ncient Egyptians believe that everything that happens in the world is controlled by the gods, so it is important not to offend them. You must bring offerings of your best produce to the temples for them. Every town has several large temples, each one the home of a god. Each pharaoh tries to outdo previous ones by building a bigger temple. Inside, priests care night and day for an image in which the god is thought to live. Ordinary people like you are not allowed inside the temples, but you know that when the crops fail or when the hot wind blows blinding sandstorms from the desert, the gods are angry.

MEET THE GODS. The four most important gods were Isis, Seth, Osiris, and Ra (see page 5), who was their king. Seth is evil, but most gods are only dangerous if offended. They must be worshipped properly.

Osiris

When the Gods Are Angry:

THE NILE doesn't rise enough at flood time, so crops can't grow and people starve.

Before / *After*

SWARMS of locusts, flying insects that gobble up crops, descend on the fields and ruin the harvest.

A CROCODILE might tip your boat while you fish on the Nile. That's the end of you!

Off-Color Days

It is not unusual for pyramid workers to be involved in serious accidents, so take care. It isn't enough just to be careful. You have to protect yourself against the evil spirits who cause such things. Some days of the year are very unlucky, when it is believed evil forces are particularly strong. These dates are listed on the calendar, so remember to check. On those days it is best to avoid bathing, making a journey, killing an ox, a goat, or a duck, lighting a fire in a house, or eating anything that lives in water. Illnesses are caused by evil spirits too, so doctors prescribe spells as well as medicine.

Other Misfortunes:

BROKEN LIMBS. If you break a leg, don't worry. Ancient Egyptian doctors are good at setting fractures.

CONSTANT COUGH? Lung diseases are common. You'll probably get one from sand in the lungs.

BLINDNESS is due to a common disease (now known to be trachoma) and means you can no longer earn a living, except perhaps as a musician.

24

To be taken three times a day after spells.

Handy Hint

Always carry an amulet—a lucky charm. This one, representing the eye of the Sun God, Ra, keeps away sickness and misfortune.

PARASITIC WORMS. Caught from polluted water, these are unwelcome guests. Some live in your limbs. Catch an end and wind it out.

OUCH! Watch where you put your feet! Scorpions living under stones have a ferocious sting.

TOOTHACHE. Apart from pulling out the tooth, there's nothing to be done. You just have to suffer.

Wrapping Up the Pharaoh

o have any chance of an afterlife you must arrange to have your body preserved when you die. If it decays your spirit will perish. In the case of a pharaoh, these arrangements are important because the well-being of Egypt relies on his union with the gods. So if you find yourself in the embalmers' workshop helping to turn smelly bodies into impressive-looking, sweet-smelling mummies, don't complain that the job is messy and makes you sick. Remember it is also a sacred process. The head embalmer wears the mask of Anubis, the god of the dead, and recites appropriate spells.

Anubis mask

Take that thing off—you're ruining the spell!

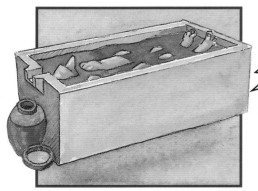

DRY THE BODY OUT completely by leaving it packed in natron (a type of salt) for 40 days.

DON'T TRY THIS AT HOME!

REMOVE THE BRAIN through the nose. Open the body, take out the insides, and fill it with sweet-smelling spices.

ANY MISSING PIECES should be replaced with wood or a wad of cloth. It won't show under the layers of linen wrappings.

26

LUCKY AMULETS are bound in wrappings and the mummy is completed by a face mask portraying the person within.

The Pyramid Is Finished!

Funerary temple

he moment has come! The pharaoh is dead and his pyramid, built with gleaming blocks of white limestone, is ready to receive him. Years of work by thousands of people, skilled and unskilled, have gone into its making. It will be his body's everlasting home. Sacred rites, performed by the temple priests daily, will keep his spirit alive forever. Pharoah's coffin is carried there in a ceremonial boat, accompanied by priests, courtiers, and professional mourners who wail loudly to express the people's grief at losing their ruler.

Farewell to the Pharaoh

MOUNTED ON A SLEDGE, the coffin is dragged along the causeway that leads from the river to the pyramid. A procession following behind bears all sorts of costly objects that will go into the pyramid for the pharaoh to use in the afterlife.

AT THE PYRAMID entrance, priests perform a ceremony that magically reawakens the dead pharaoh's senses.

Handy Hint ?

Cover the pyramid entrance with casing blocks, to baffle thieves seeking to steal the riches buried with the pharaoh.

Causeway

They got that pyramid finished just in time.

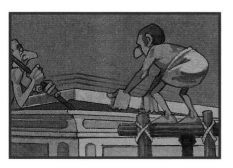

IN THE BURIAL CHAMBER the priests lower the coffin into its sarcophagus. Assistants set its massive stone lid in place.

THE PYRAMID is sealed with giant stone slabs dropped into place by the last people to leave.

A NEW PYRAMID TO BUILD. Don't count on getting a break. The new pharaoh wants work started on his—at once!

29

Glossary

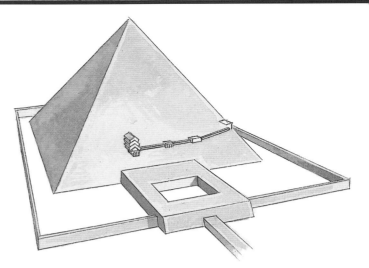

Amulet A lucky charm.

Barracks A set of buildings used to lodge soldiers or workers.

Canal An artificial waterway, made by digging a channel to receive water from elsewhere.

Capstone The top piece of a pyramid.

Casing blocks High-quality limestone blocks used to cover the outside of the pyramid.

Causeway A raised roadway built over water.

Claustrophobic To cause a panicky feeling of being shut in, especially in small spaces.

Conscript A person forced to do certain work.

Dolerite A dark, fine-grained, very hard rock.

Embalmer A person who preserves dead bodies with scented oils and spices before their funeral.

Grid A network of lines crossing at right angles, forming squares.

Lever A long wooden bar used to pry up or dislodge a heavy object.

Linen A fabric woven from the fibers of the flax plant. The best Ancient Egyptian linen was very valuable.

Mason Someone who builds or works with stone.

Mattock A digging tool.

Mortuary temple The temple in which priests performed the daily rituals that kept the dead pharaoh's spirit alive. It was built against one wall of a pyramid.

Mummification The process by which the body is dried out and preserved.

Natron A type of salt found in the ground in some parts of the world.

Parasitic To live on, or in, another living thing and feed on it.

Portcullis A heavy door which closes by dropping from a recess above.

Quarry A place where stone for building is cut out of the ground.

Quartz A very common hard mineral, found as rock or in sand.

Reservoir A tank or artificial pool in which large quantities of water can be stored.

Sarcophagus An outer coffin made of stone.

Scribe An official who is responsible for keeping written records.

Shrine A place, such as a recess in a wall, where the image of a god is kept.

Slurry Thin, sloppy mud.

Trachoma A disease of the eye which is a widespread cause of blindness in Africa and Asia.

Vizier A high-ranking official in a pharaoh's staff.

31

Index

The City of the Dead

A pharaoh's pyramid did not stand alone; it was surrounded by many other buildings, as shown in this view of the pyramids at Giza. In addition to the mortuary temple and small side temples, there were often one or more smaller pyramids. Archeologists used to think that these were the pyramids of queens, but now it is believed that they may have held jars containing the pharaoh's organs. Around the pyramid, the low, flat tombs of the pharaoh's relations and courtiers were laid out in avenues. In the foreground is the Great Pyramid, built in about 2566 B.C. by Khufu (or Cheops), a pharaoh of the Fourth Dynasty. The middle pyramid is that of his son Khafre (Chephren). Beyond that is the pyramid of Menkaure (Mycerinus), who may have been Khafre's brother or son.

In 1954, archeologists found a sealed boat pit near the Great Pyramid. Inside were 1,224 pieces of wood, along with ropes for rigging, baskets, and matting. It took ten years to figure out how this, the world's oldest construction kit, fitted together.

The Sphinx, an enormous man-headed lion, lies crouched near the valley temple of Khafre. In Egyptian mythology, the lion was a guardian of sacred places.

Top Egyptian Pharaohs

• **Hatshepsut** (reigned ca. 1479–1458 B.C.) was one of the few female pharaohs. She took charge of Egypt with the support of the high priest and other officials. During her reign of about 22 years, the country prospered. She encouraged trade, built impressive temples, and restored many others. Her magnificent mortuary temple is at Deir el-Bahri. After her death, her stepson Thutmose III became pharaoh.

• **Thutmose III** (reigned 1479–1425 B.C.) has been called "the Napoleon of ancient Egypt." For about the first 22 years of his reign, he ruled with Hatshepsut. A military genius, he was a national hero respected throughout Egyptian history. He is well known for his many buildings and monuments, including great obelisks (tall, four-sided tapering towers).

• **Tutankhamun** (reigned ca. 1336–1327 B.C.) became pharaoh at the age of nine. His uncle ruled for him while he was a boy. Tut married Ankhesenamun and died at age 18. He is famous today because so many of his possessions have survived. His body was damaged during excavation, and the cause of his early death is uncertain.

• **Ramses II** (reigned ca. 1279–1213 B.C.), called Ramses the Great, ruled for 67 years, at a time when the average person in Egypt lived only to about 40. It is said that Ramses lived for over 80 years. Famed as a builder and a warrior, he had more than a dozen wives and more than 100 children.

The mummified head of Ramses II and an X-ray of his skull

Howard Carter and Lord Carnarvon

Lord Carnarvon

British archeologist Howard Carter was employed by English aristocrat Lord Carnarvon, who had gone to Egypt for his health and enjoyed doing some excavating. Carter's job was to find promising sites for Carnarvon to explore. Working together from 1907, they made many finds. In 1922, they made the most famous archeological discovery ever: the tomb of Tutankhamun.

Did You Know?

Four months after the opening of the tomb, Lord Carnarvon died from an infected mosquito bite, giving rise to the idea of the "curse of the pharaohs." It was said that at the time of his death, all the lights in Cairo went out and at the same instant, in England, Carnarvon's dog dropped dead. The supposed curse did not touch Howard Carter, however. He survived for another 17 years. He completed the task of clearing the tomb, and died from natural causes in 1939.